MAPS and MAPPING

RESOURCES

By Susan Hoe

Science and curriculum consultant:
Debra Voege, M.A., science curriculum resource teacher

Gareth Stevens
Publishing

Please visit our web site at www.garethstevens.com
For a free catalog describing our list of high-quality books, call 1-800-542-2595 (USA) or 1-800-387-3178 (Canada).
Our fax: 1-877-542-2596

Library of Congress Cataloging-in-Publication Data available upon request from publisher.

ISBN-10: 0-8368-9206-2   ISBN-13: 978-0-8368-9206-2 (lib. bdg.)
ISBN-10: 0-8368-9333-6   ISBN-13: 978-0-8368-9333-5 (softcover)

This edition first published in 2009 by
Gareth Stevens Publishing
A Weekly Reader® Company
1 Reader's Digest Road
Pleasantville, NY 10570-7000 USA

This U.S. edition copyright © 2009 by Gareth Stevens, Inc. Original edition copyright © 2008 by ticktock Media Ltd. First published in Great Britain in 2008 by ticktock Media Ltd., Unit 2, Orchard Business Centre, North Farm Road, Tunbridge Wells, Kent, TN2 3XF

Gareth Stevens Senior Managing Editor: Lisa M. Herrington
Gareth Stevens Creative Director: Lisa Donovan
Gareth Stevens Art Director: Ken Crossland
Gareth Stevens Associate Editor: Amanda Hudson

Picture credits (t=top; b=bottom; c=center; l=left; r=right):
Peter Bull Art Studio: 14, 31b; Dean Conger/Corbis: 20br; Getmapping PLC: 24tc; Image100/SuperStock: 7b; iStock: 17tl, 19t, 19br, 21b, 22t, 25b, 27 (oil barrel); Jupiter Images: 2, 6t, 13tr; www.mapart.co.uk: 7t, 12, 13b, 17b, 18, 22b, 23, 26, 30; Iain Masterton/Alamy: 17tr; MIXA. Co., Ltd./Alamy: 4t; Ulli Seer/Getty Images: 5t; Shutterstock: 6b, 10all, 13tl, 15 all, 19tr, 19bl, 24tl, 24b, 25t, 25c, 27 all (except oil barrel); Justin Spain: 4c, 9 all, 21t, 31t; Hayley Terry: 5b, 11; Tim Thirlaway: 28, 29; ticktock Media archive: 4b, 8; Steve Vidler/SuperStock: 17cr, 20bl.

Printed in the United States of America

1 2 3 4 5 6 7 8 9 10 09 08

Contents

Words in **bold** are defined in the glossary.

What Is a Map?

A **map** is a special drawing. A map shows a certain place or area. The place or area is drawn as if seen from above.

This place can be as big as the whole world. Or it can be as small as your local candy store!

Making a Map of an Island

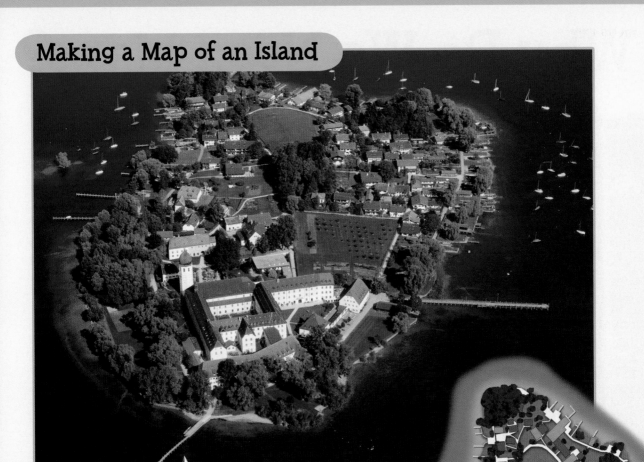

Map Key

 Trees/woods

 Roads/footpaths

 Gray-roofed building

 Red-roofed building

 Pier

 Garden

Maps help us find things as if we were directly above them.

In this book, we are going to see how maps show where things are made. But first let's look at some of the ways that maps can help us.

Find red-roofed buildings on the map.

Now look for red-roofed buildings in the photo.

5

Why Do We Need Maps?

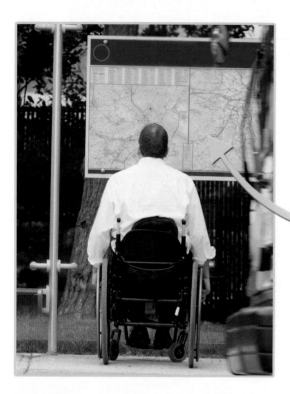

Maps help us find our way around. They give us all kinds of information about where we live!

A map can help you get from one place to another. It can show you where you are. It can show you where to go and how to get there.

Weather Map of the United States

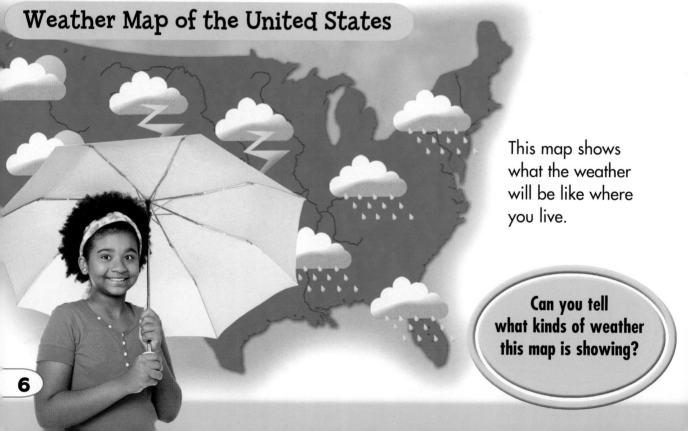

This map shows what the weather will be like where you live.

Can you tell what kinds of weather this map is showing?

World Map

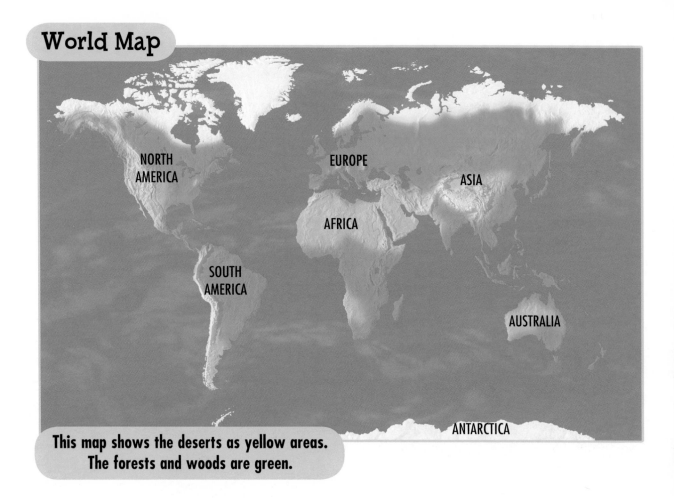

NORTH
AMERICA

EUROPE

ASIA

AFRICA

SOUTH
AMERICA

AUSTRALIA

ANTARCTICA

**This map shows the deserts as yellow areas.
The forests and woods are green.**

Maps teach us important facts about places.
We can learn about places close to home
or far away.

Maps can show whether land is flat or
has hills. We can learn what kinds of
things are made in certain places.
Maps can also show which animals
live in certain places.

Maps are handy and easy to use. They
can show us huge areas in a small amount
of space. We can take them just about
anywhere!

Mapping a Candy Store

A map shows a place as if you were looking down on it. That place can be your country or your town. It can even be your favorite candy store!

A 3-D candy store

This candy store is a **three-dimensional (3-D)** space. The store and the things in the store are solid. They have length, width, and **depth**.

A 2-D Map

A map is a flat, or **two-dimensional (2-D)**, drawing of a space. On a map, all of the objects in the store look flat. They have length and width only. Let's see how we can make a solid room look flat.

To create a map, all the flat shapes are drawn on a piece of paper.

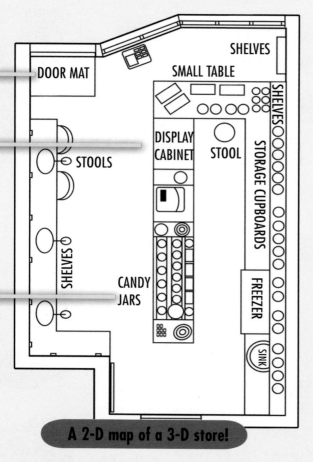

DOOR MAT

STOOLS

SHELVES

SHELVES

SMALL TABLE

DISPLAY CABINET

STOOL

STORAGE CUPBOARDS

SHELVES

CANDY JARS

FREEZER

SINK

A 2-D map of a 3-D store!

This map shows you how to find everything in the store.

Find the stools.

Find the freezer.

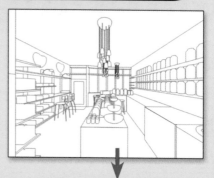

This 3-D drawing of the store was made from photos.

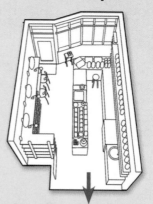

Pretend you are able to float above the candy store. Imagine looking down on it.

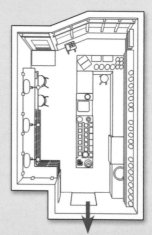

To create the 2-D map, draw all of the candy store shapes that you see from above. Make the flat shapes on a piece of paper.

Mapping a Mall

You just saw how to map a candy store. You can also use maps to show larger areas. When you look at a map of a shopping mall, you can see all the stores. The map tells you where to find each one.

A 3-D view of a mall

This photo shows many shops in a mall. Without a map, it can be hard to find the right one!

Your Mall: A Window to the World!

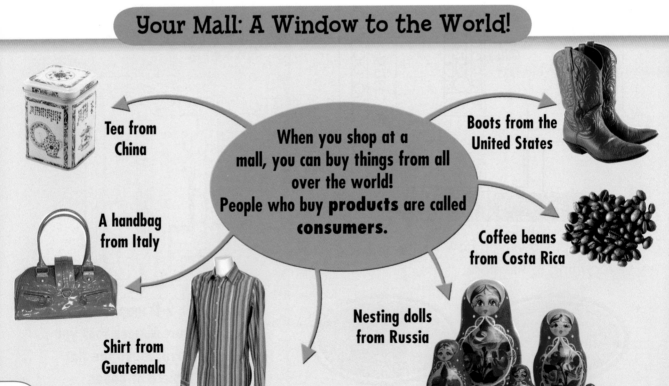

When you shop at a mall, you can buy things from all over the world!
People who buy **products** are called **consumers.**

Tea from China

Boots from the United States

A handbag from Italy

Coffee beans from Costa Rica

Shirt from Guatemala

Nesting dolls from Russia

A 2-D Map of a Mall

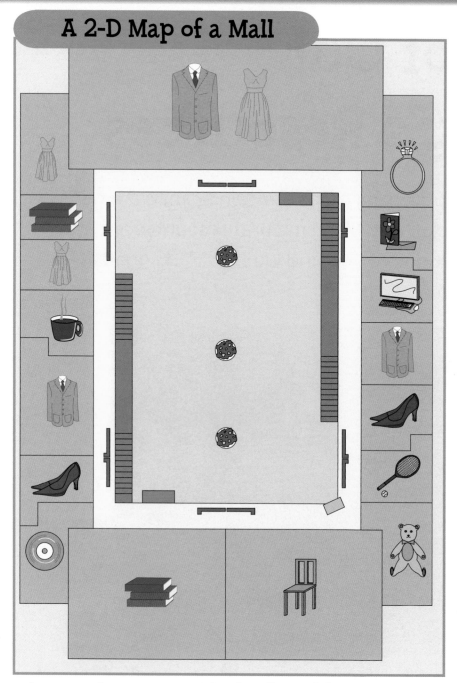

Map Key

- ◎ Music store
- Men's clothing store
- Women's clothing store
- Computer store
- Bookstore
- Jewelry store
- Department store
- Toy store
- Greeting card store
- Furniture store
- Coffee shop
- Sporting goods store
- Shoe store
- Seating area
- Elevator
- Mall map
- Escalator
- Walkway
- Plants

This map shows stores on the first floor of the mall. It uses **symbols** that stand for each store. The map has a key. This **map key** is also called a legend. It shows what each symbol means.

Find the toy store.

How many shoe stores are on the first floor?

11

A Map of Our Country's Resources

The United States grows many crops. Certain animals are raised to provide food and clothing. Many **natural resources** are also found here. These include coal, oil, and lumber. Many **goods** are made in factories, too.

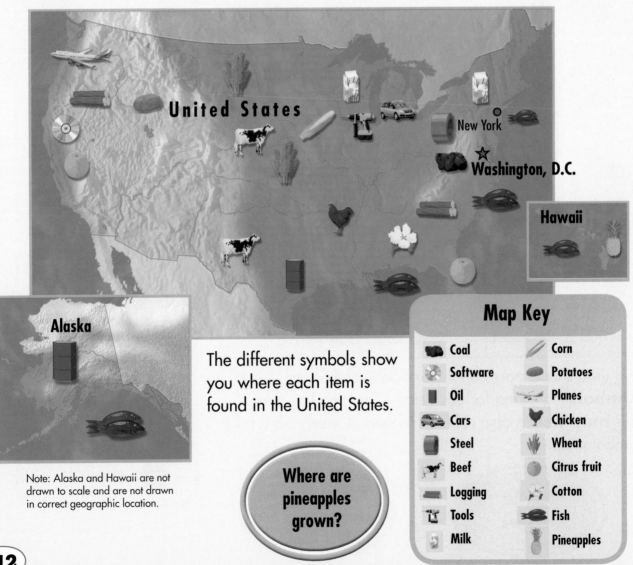

Alaska

Note: Alaska and Hawaii are not drawn to scale and are not drawn in correct geographic location.

The different symbols show you where each item is found in the United States.

Where are pineapples grown?

Map Key

Coal	Corn
Software	Potatoes
Oil	Planes
Cars	Chicken
Steel	Wheat
Beef	Citrus fruit
Logging	Cotton
Tools	Fish
Milk	Pineapples

Corn is a crop that has many uses. It can be used to feed farm animals. Its green stalks can be used to make paper. When it rots, it can be used to create fuel for cars. For most people, though, corn is just fun to eat!

What Is Scale?

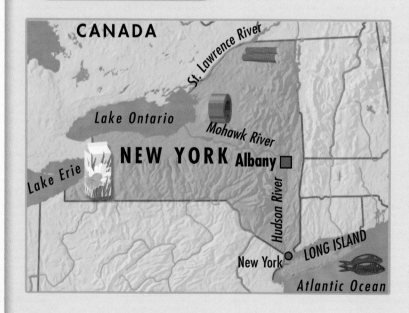

CANADA

St. Lawrence River

Lake Ontario

Mohawk River

NEW YORK Albany ☐

Lake Erie

Hudson River

New York ○ LONG ISLAND

Atlantic Ocean

A map cannot be as big as the area it shows. Mapmakers must fit all of the real area onto paper. Everything must be drawn much smaller than it is in real life. This is called drawing to **scale**.

Look at the map on page 14. Then look at the map to the left. You can more easily see **land features**, such as rivers, on the map of New York state.

What resource is shown closest to Long Island?

What kind of drink is produced in New York?

Mapping Our World

The United States is part of North America. North America is a large land area called a continent. Maps of the world have seven continents. The continents are North America, South America, Africa, Europe, Asia, Australia, and Antarctica. Earth also has many large bodies of water. These are called oceans and seas.

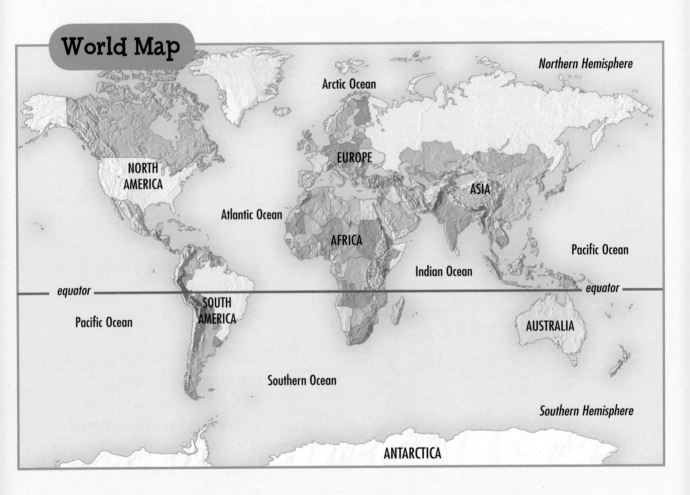

World Map

Northern Hemisphere

Arctic Ocean

EUROPE

NORTH AMERICA

ASIA

Atlantic Ocean

AFRICA

Pacific Ocean

Indian Ocean

equator — SOUTH AMERICA — equator

Pacific Ocean

AUSTRALIA

Southern Ocean

Southern Hemisphere

ANTARCTICA

The equator is an imaginary line. It divides Earth into two halves. One half is the Northern Hemisphere. The other half is the Southern Hemisphere. North America is north of the equator.

Across the Continents—a World of Goods

Continents are divided into countries. Sometimes, a country sells its goods to another country. That is called **exporting**. Sometimes, a country buys goods from another country. That is called **importing**. Many countries export their goods to the United States.

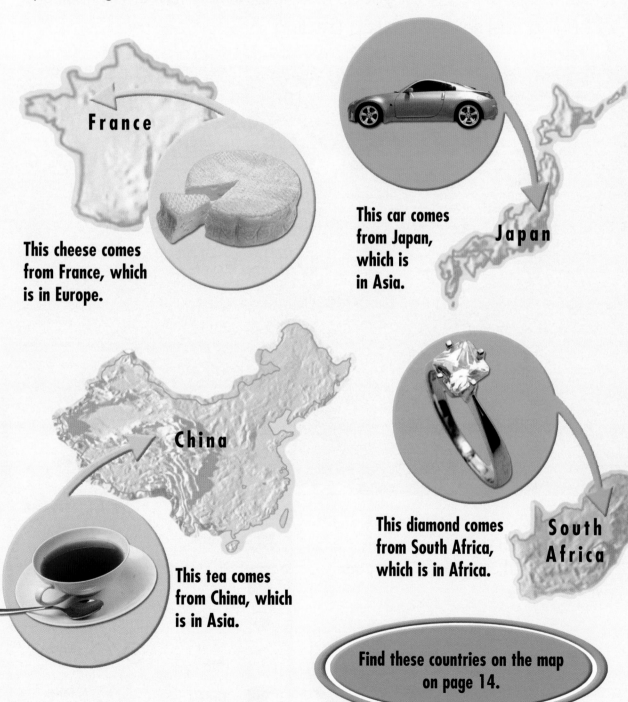

France

This cheese comes from France, which is in Europe.

This car comes from Japan, which is in Asia.

Japan

China

This tea comes from China, which is in Asia.

This diamond comes from South Africa, which is in Africa.

South Africa

Find these countries on the map on page 14.

A World Trade Map

The United States sells, or exports, goods to other countries. It also buys, or imports, goods from other countries. This type of buying and selling is called trading.

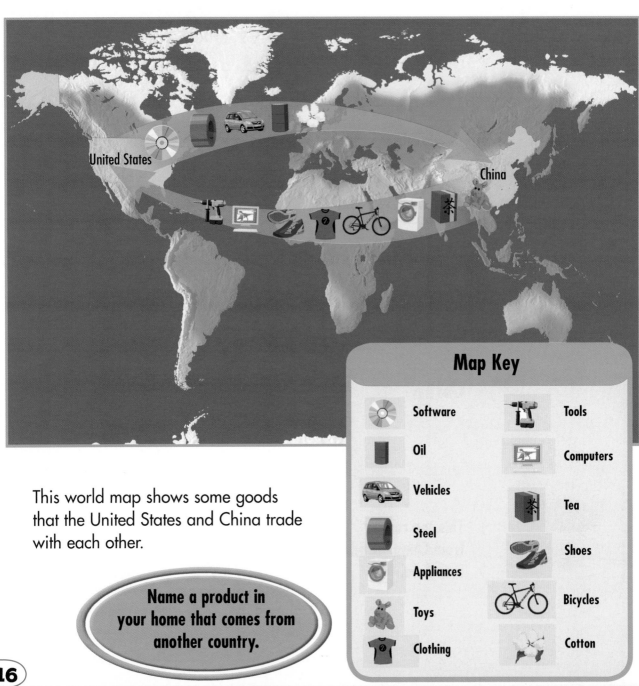

This world map shows some goods that the United States and China trade with each other.

Name a product in your home that comes from another country.

Map Key

Software		Tools	
Oil		Computers	
Vehicles		Tea	
Steel		Shoes	
Appliances		Bicycles	
Toys		Cotton	
Clothing			

Large cargo ships are called **freighters**. They carry goods between the United States and other countries.

Cars from other countries are unloaded from ships in U.S. ports. The cars will be bought and used by Americans.

The Silk Road

People from different continents have traded goods with one another for hundreds of years. One of the oldest **trade routes** was called the Silk Road. It connected Asia with parts of Europe.

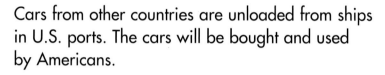

Silk fabrics from China

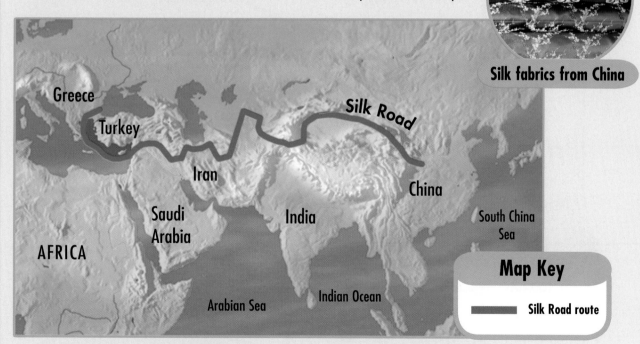

Greece

Turkey

Silk Road

Iran

China

Saudi
Arabia

India

South China
Sea

AFRICA

Arabian Sea

Indian Ocean

Map Key

———— Silk Road route

People traveled on the Silk Road between China and places in Europe. They carried pretty silk material. They also carried gold and spices.

Mapping Goods From China

China is the largest country on the continent of Asia. There are three seas along China's eastern and southern **coastline**. The seas are the Yellow Sea, East China Sea, and South China Sea.

China is a big country. Its climate and land features are different all around the country. China has many different kinds of land. It grows all kinds of crops. China also has many natural resources and makes many products.

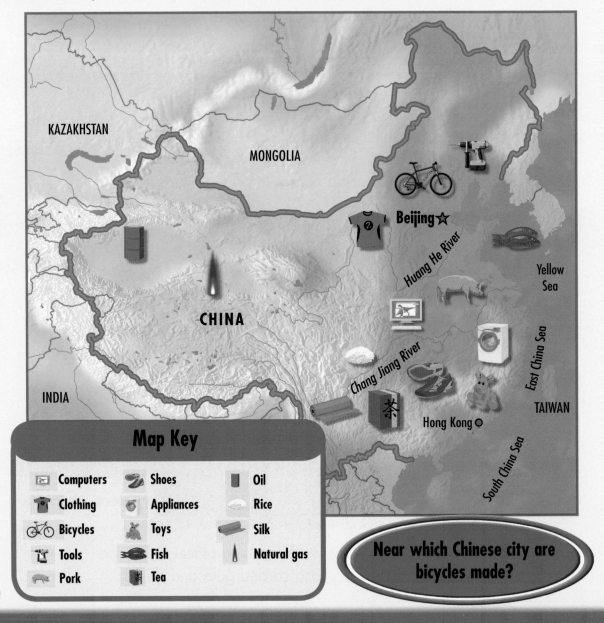

Map Key

Computers	Shoes	Oil
Clothing	Appliances	Rice
Bicycles	Toys	Silk
Tools	Fish	Natural gas
Pork	Tea	

Near which Chinese city are bicycles made?

18

The mountains in China (left) are rich in **minerals**. You can find gold, iron, and coal there. These minerals can be used to make many products. They are used in jewelry, metal goods, and fuel.

Tea fields are planted on the warm and rainy hillsides. Rice grows in paddies where there is lots of water (right). In central and eastern farmlands, thread from the silkworm is gathered.

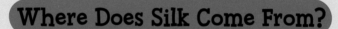

Where Does Silk Come From?

Silkworms are caterpillars. They weave their cocoons out of a single silk thread. This thread can be used to make silk material.

Mapping a Tea Farm in China

China exports tea to other countries. The tea is grown on large farms, called plantations. Many people work on tea farms in China.

Tea is planted on hillsides. Workers walk along dirt roads to get to the fields. Tall trees help protect the tea bushes from strong winds. On the edge of this field is a tea factory. The picked tea leaves are taken there to be prepared for **market**.

This worker picks the tea leaves. She puts them in large baskets.

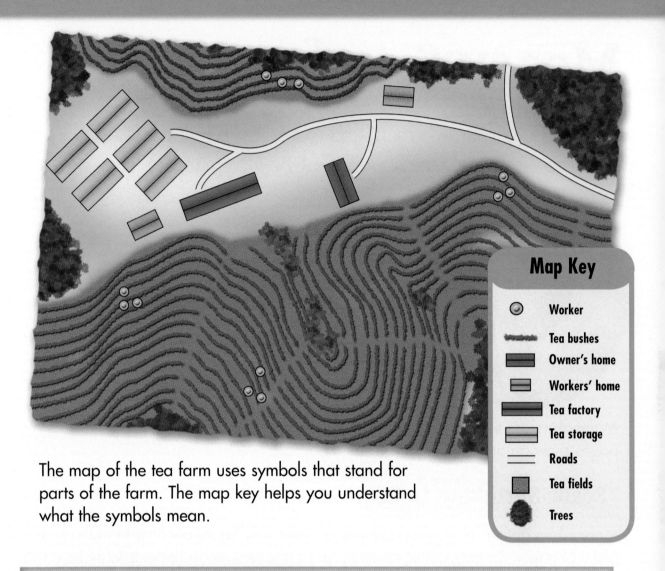

The map of the tea farm uses symbols that stand for parts of the farm. The map key helps you understand what the symbols mean.

Map Key

◎	Worker
	Tea bushes
	Owner's home
	Workers' home
	Tea factory
	Tea storage
═══	Roads
	Tea fields
	Trees

Export and Import

China exports thousands of tons of tea to the United States. But what does it import from the United States?

To build tall buildings, China imports crane machines from the United States.

Measuring for Maps

Before you can draw a map, you must figure out the size and shape of the area. This means figuring out how to measure large areas.

This man uses special equipment to measure distances between points.

Mapmakers use their measurements to draw their maps. The maps on these pages show an amusement park.

Scale: Shrinking to Fit

Mapmakers gather all their measurements. Then they figure out how to fit them onto a piece of paper. So they shrink, or scale down, the real measurements to make a map.

0	50 feet
	15 meters

This map shows a fairly large area. It uses a scale of 50 feet (15 meters). Many objects can be seen, but they are quite small.

Different scales can be used to map the same area. A different scale can change what you see. Some maps show large areas on a sheet of paper. Other maps show smaller areas, so the same objects look bigger and have more features.

The map scale is like a ruler. It shows the connection between distance on the map and distance on the ground. This way you can figure out real distances on the map.

0   25 feet

8 meters

This map shows a smaller area than the first map. This map uses a scale of 25 feet (8 m). You see fewer objects on this map, but they seem closer.

0   15 feet

5 meters

This map has the largest scale. It shows an even smaller area. You see fewer objects, but they seem even closer.

Mapping With Computers

Many years ago, people had to travel to figure out the shape of the land. Today, mapmakers use computer equipment.

Mapmakers can take many photographs of the ground from an airplane.

This photograph shows the ground as seen from the airplane.

Pictures and measurements are taken from an airplane and sent to computers. The computers use the pictures to draw maps.

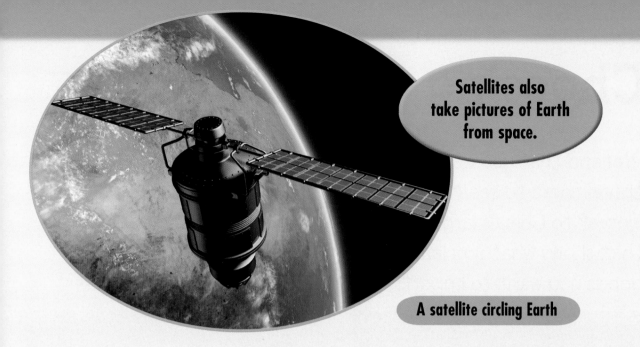

Satellites also take pictures of Earth from space.

A satellite circling Earth

Pictures are taken from space, too. The pictures are sent back to Earth. They are put together to make full pictures of our planet, like the one shown here. These pictures can then be turned into maps.

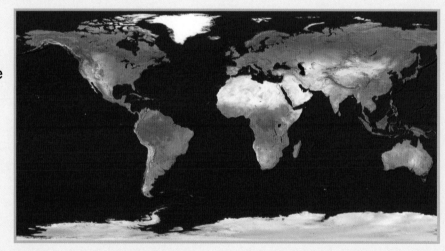

Changing Maps

Satellites can produce road maps that help you find your way. These maps change as you move. The maps are called **GPS (Global Positioning System)** maps.

A GPS map at work in a car

Choosing Goods to Ship

Pretend that you want to import goods from China. You must travel there to see them. Try to figure out which goods are closest to China's largest cities. Here's how you can create a map that shows what you learn. This map shows where to find the goods you want to import!

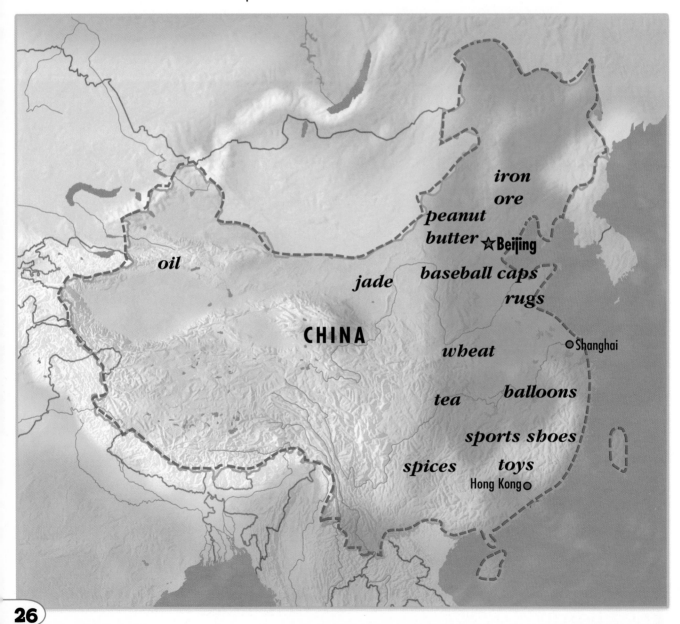

How to Make a Map of Goods in China

1. Copy the map of China on page 26 onto a blank sheet of paper. You can also use thin paper to trace the map.

2. Now make a map key. Include goods from the list below. Draw pictures of these goods in your map key.

Map Key

balloons	toys	sports shoes	wheat
oil	spices	peanut butter	rugs
jade	iron ore	tea	baseball caps

3. The map on page 26 shows some places where these goods are made in China. Use this map as a guide. Draw pictures of goods on your map of China. Put your pictures in places where the goods are made.

4. Which goods are located closest to Beijing, Shanghai, and Hong Kong? Which are farthest from these cities?

Making Your Own Mall Map

Now you can design your dream shopping mall with all your favorite stores. Make a map key so your friends can see all the great things in your mall.

> **What is the shape of your mall?**

> **What can you buy in the stores at your mall? Is there a toy store or a bookstore? Is there a store for games?**

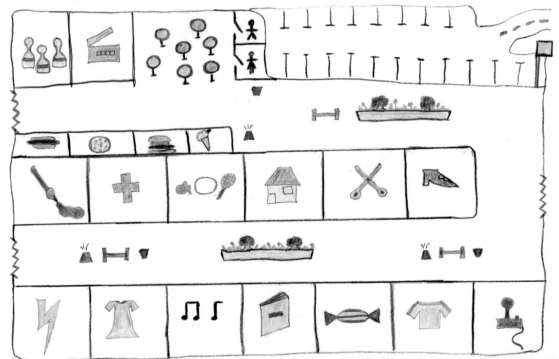

Gabby's Great Mall

> **What kinds of food does your mall sell? Is there an ice cream shop? Is there a pizza place?**

> **Will your mall have restrooms and water fountains? Will it have indoor plants and trash cans?**

Step 1

Draw the shape of your mall on a piece of paper. Be sure to show where the entrance is.

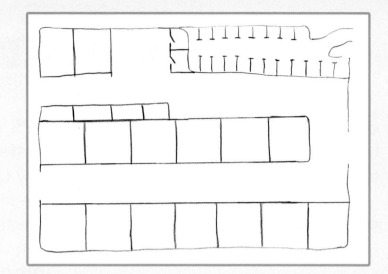

Step 2

Make up symbols for all of the shops. Make symbols for the other items you want to include on your map. Be sure to leave enough space between the symbols.

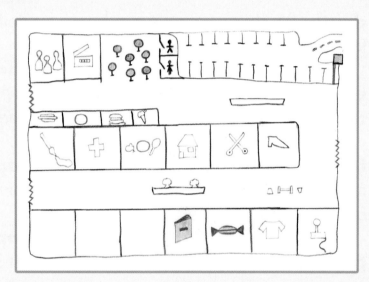

Step 3

Color your mall map and give your mall a name!

Step 4

Make your map key using the symbols on your map.

 Map Key

Bowling alley Doors Water fountain Sporting goods Music store

Movie theater Hot dogs Bench Housewares Bookstore

Food court Pizza Indoor plants Hairdresser Candy store

Restrooms Burgers Art shop Shoe shop Men's clothing

Parking lot Trash can Ice cream Pharmacy Women's clothing Electrical appliances Games store

Glossary

coastline: the line that forms a border between land and a body of water

consumers: people who buy or use things

depth: the distance measured from top to bottom or front to back

exporting: selling goods to another country

freighters: large ships used to move small and large goods from one country to another

goods: items that can be sold

GPS (Global Positioning System): an instrument that shows how to get to a place. In a moving car, the instrument shows the driver directions on a screen.

importing: buying goods from another country

land features: natural areas on Earth. These include mountains, rivers, forests, and deserts.

map: a picture or chart showing features of an area

map key: the space on a map that shows the meaning of any pictures or colors on the map

market: a place where things are sold

minerals: kinds of material in nature that are neither an animal nor a vegetable

natural resources: materials that come from Earth and are used by people. Coal, oil, water, fish, and trees are some natural resources.

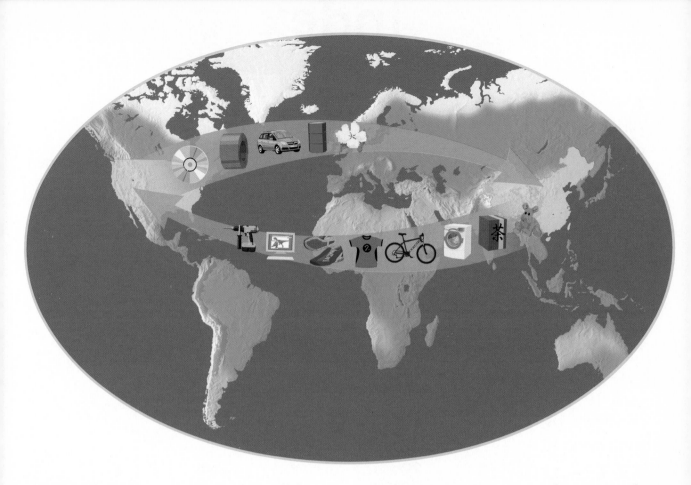

products: items made to be sold

satellites: objects sent into space that circle and study Earth or other bodies in space. They then send information back to Earth.

scale: the amount by which the measurement of an area is shrunk to fit on a map. The map scale is a drawing or symbol that tells how to measure distances on a map.

symbols: pictures or drawings that stand for different things

three-dimensional (3-D): appearing as a solid thing that has length, width, and depth

trade routes: travel paths used to carry goods between countries

two-dimensional (2-D): appearing as a flat shape with only length and width

Index